HOUSE (

European Union Committee

38th Report of Session 2006–07

Current Developments in European Foreign Policy

Report with Evidence

Ordered to be printed 23 October 2007 and published 30 October 2007

Published by the Authority of the House of Lords

London : The Stationery Office Limited
£6.50

HL Paper 183

The European Union Committee

The European Union Committee is appointed by the House of Lords "to consider European Union documents and other matters relating to the European Union". The Committee has seven Sub-Committees which are:

Economic and Financial Affairs, and International Trade (Sub-Committee A)
Internal Market (Sub-Committee B)
Foreign Affairs, Defence and Development Policy (Sub-Committee C)
Environment and Agriculture (Sub-Committee D)
Law and Institutions (Sub-Committee E)
Home Affairs (Sub-Committee F)
Social and Consumer Affairs (Sub-Committee G)

Our Membership

The Members of the European Union Committee are:

Lord Blackwell
Lord Bowness
Lord Brown of Eaton-under-Heywood
Baroness Cohen of Pimlico
Lord Freeman
Lord Geddes
Lord Grenfell (Chairman)
Lord Harrison
Lord Kerr of Kinlochard

Lord Maclennan of Rogart
Lord Marlesford
Lord Powell of Bayswater
Lord Roper
Lord Sewel
Baroness Symons of Vernham Dean
Baroness Thomas of Walliswood
Lord Tomlinson
Lord Wright of Richmond

The Members of the Sub-Committee which carried out this inquiry (Foreign Affairs, Defence and Development Policy, Sub-Committee C) are:

Lord Anderson of Swansea
Lord Boyce
Lord Chidgey
Lord Crickhowell
Lord Hamilton of Epsom
Lord Hannay of Chiswick

Lord Lea of Crondall
Lord Roper (Chairman)
Lord Swinfen
Baroness Symons of Vernham Dean
Lord Tomlinson

Information about the Committee

The reports and evidence of the Committee are published by and available from The Stationery Office. For information freely available on the web, our homepage is:
http://www.parliament.uk/parliamentary_committees/lords_eu_select_committee.cfm
There you will find many of our publications, along with press notices, details of membership and forthcoming meetings, and other information about the ongoing work of the Committee and its Sub-Committees, each of which has its own homepage.

General Information

General information about the House of Lords and its Committees, including guidance to witnesses, details of current inquiries and forthcoming meetings is on the internet at
http://www.parliament.uk/about_lords/about_lords.cfm

Contacts for the European Union Committee

Contact details for individual Sub-Committees are given on the website.
General correspondence should be addressed to the Clerk of the European Union Committee, Committee Office, House of Lords, London, SW1A OPW
The telephone number for general enquiries is 020 7219 5791.
The Committee's email address is euclords@parliament.uk

CONTENTS

Oral Evidence

Mr Jim Murphy MP, Minister of State, Europe, Foreign and Commonwealth Office;
Mr Martin Shearman, Head of Common Foreign and Security Policy Group;
Mr Alan Parfitt, Leader of research Analysts on CIS Energy and Central Asia

NOTE: References in the text of the report are as follows:
(Q) refers to a question in oral evidence
(p) refers to a page of written evidence

Current Developments in European Foreign Policy

REPORT

1. The Committee asked the Minister for Europe, Mr Jim Murphy MP, to give evidence on the most recent developments in European Foreign Policy. We thank the Minister for his time

2. In this Report we make available, for the information of the House, the oral evidence given to Sub-Committee C (Foreign Affairs, Defence and Development Policy) by the Minister for Europe, accompanied by Mr Martin Shearman, Head of the Common Foreign and Security Policy Group (CFSP), and Mr Alan Parfitt, Leader of Research Analysts on CIS Energy and Central Asia, on 25 July 2007; and the correspondence from the Minister.

3. Key topics in the evidence are:

EU/Africa

- The EU/Africa relationship as a partnership, the need for specific outcomes, the importance of properly functioning domestic governance (QQ 1, 3, 7);

- Aid policy, aid and trade (Q 2);

- The African peer review group mechanism (Q 4);

- The need for good communications and transport in Africa (QQ 5, 6);

- AU-EU relations (QQ 7, 8);

- Africa's relations with China (Q 8);

- The appointment of an EU Special Representative for Africa (Q 9);

ESDP

- The EU's civilian capabilities for crisis management and new headline goals (QQ 10, 13–15);

- Hybrid operations and cooperation with other organisations such as NATO, the UN, the AU and the OSCE (Q 11);

- The question of Turkey (Q 12);

Central Asia Strategy

- The Rule of Law Initiative (p 9);

- The EU's strategy on Central Asia as a basis for meeting the goals of the EU's external energy policy, the security of supplies, and the St Petersburg declaration (QQ 16–19);

- The Central Asia investment climate (QQ 19, 20);

- The need to differentiate between different Central Asian States (Q 21);

Kosovo

- The prospective operation in Kosovo (QQ 11, 23);
- Kosovo independence (QQ 22, 24);
- Russian concerns (Q 23);
- Action at the UN (Q 25);

European Neighbourhood Policy (ENP)

- The development of individual plans for different countries (Q 26);
- Plans for strengthening the Mediterranean dimension of the ENP (p 9).

APPENDIX 1: SUB-COMMITTEE C (FOREIGN AFFAIRS, DEFENCE AND DEVELOPMENT POLICY)

The Members of the Sub-Committee which conducted this Inquiry were:

Lord Anderson of Swansea
Lord Boyce
Lord Chidgey
Lord Crickhowell
Lord Hamilton of Epsom
Lord Hannay of Chiswick
Lord Lea of Crondall
Lord Roper (Chairman)
Lord Swinfen
Baroness Symons of Vernham Dean
Lord Tomlinson

Declaration of Interests

A full list of Members' interest can be found in the Register of Lords Interests:

http://www.publications.parliament.uk/pa/ld/ldreg.htm

APPENDIX 2: REPORTS

Recent Reports from the Select Committee

Evidence from the Minister for Europe on the Outcome of the December European Council (4th Report, Session 2006–07, HL Paper 31)

Government Responses: Session 2004–05 (6th Report, Session 2006–07, HL Paper 38)

The Commission's 2007 Legislative and Work Programme (7th Report, Session 2006–07, HL Paper 42)

Evidence from the Ambassador of the Federal Republic of Germany on the German Presidency (10th Report, Session 2006–07, HL Paper 56)

The Commission's Annual Policy Strategy for 2008 (23rd Report, Session 2006–07, HL Paper 123)

Further Enlargement of the EU: Follow-up Report (24th Report, Session 2006–07, HL Paper 125)

Evidence from the Minister for Europe on the June European Council and the 2007 Inter-Governmental Conference (28th Report, Session 2006–07, HL Paper 142)

Evidence from the Ambassador of Portugal on the Priorities of the Portuguese Presidency (29th Report, Session 2006–07, HL Paper 143)

Session 2006–2007 Reports prepared by Sub-Committee C

Current Developments in European Defence Policy (1st Report, HL Paper 17)

Current Developments in European Foreign Policy (16th Report, HL Paper 76)

The EU and the Middle East Peace Process (26th Report, HL Paper 132)

Current Developments in European Foreign Policy: Kosovo (32nd Report, HL Paper 154)

Current Developments in European Defence Policy (34th Report, HL Paper 161)

Session 2005–2006 Reports prepared by Sub-Committee C

The European Union's Role at the Millennium Review Summit (11th Report, HL Paper 35)

Review of Scrutiny: Common Foreign and Security Policy (19th Report, HL Paper 100)

Current Developments in European Foreign Policy (26th Report, HL Paper 124)

Current Developments in European Defence Policy (27th Report, HL Paper 125)

Seventh Framework Programme for Research (33rd Report, HL Paper 182) (prepared jointly with Sub-Committee B)

The EU and Africa: Towards a Strategic Partnership (34th Report, HL Paper 206)

Current Developments in European Defence Policy (35th Report, HL Paper 209)

Current Developments in European Foreign Policy (43rd Report, HL Paper 228)

Europe in the World (48th Report, HL Paper 268)

The EU and Africa: Follow-up Report (49th Report, HL Paper 269)

Minutes of Evidence

TAKEN BEFORE THE SELECT COMMTTEE ON THE EUROPEAN UNION
(SUB-COMMITTEE C)

WEDNESDAY 25 JULY 2007

Present   Anderson of Swansea, L   Lea of Crondall, L
Crickhowell, L   Roper, L (Chairman)
Hannay of Chiswick, L   Swinfen, L

Examination of Witnesses

Witnesses: Mr Jim Murphy, a Member of the House of Commons, Minister of State for Europe, Foreign & Commonwealth Office, Mr Martin Shearman, Head of the Common Foreign and Security Policy Group (CFSP), and Mr Alan Parfitt, Leader of Research Analysts on CIS Energy and Central Asia, examined.

Chairman: Minister, thank you very much indeed for coming to meet Sub-Committee C today. We used to see your predecessor twice a year to discuss the six months work, particularly in the General Affairs and External Relations Council and matters of foreign and defence policy which came up at the European Council meetings, but we also with him, on one occasion at least, saw him on a specific topic—he came to see us on Kosovo—and we hope that there are specific things in future we might be able to talk to you again about that, but at the moment what I would like to do is to say that we are very pleased that you are here with Mr Parfitt and Mr Shearman and that we have some questions, which I think you have got some ideas about. I would like to start by asking Lord Crickhowell if he would like to start.

Q1 *Lord Crickhowell:* Can we start on the EU-Africa summit. In what ways will the Joint EU-Africa strategy, which we expect to be adopted in the summit in December, represent a step-change in the level of cooperation compared with the current EU partnership with Africa?

Mr Murphy: My Lord Chairman, thank you for your warm welcome. I am happy and eager to see just how we can have a close working relationship on the issues that we discuss today, or indeed, if your Lordships were so minded, to have specific hearings or conversations about events on any of the areas I am responsible for as they unfold. In terms of the specific point raised by Lord Crickhowell, two of the things which I think it is important to emphasise are that in terms of the African Union what it should be about, I think, as it evolves—and I spoke to the Portuguese Foreign Minister at lunchtime about this—is a much greater sense of it being a partnership rather than the EU saying, "Here's what we're doing and Africa, as a continent or a collection of nations, accepting that in some sort of sense of gratitude." That would be important. The other thing which the United

Kingdom is very keen to achieve is some specific outcomes, rather than simply a well-worded document. This partnership should add some value based on specific outcomes, and for the United Kingdom that would be issues predominantly about governance, domestic governance, and rule of law issues, as well as continuing economic reform where that can be achieved.

Q2 *Lord Crickhowell:* I want to follow that up, if I may, with really a question about aid policy. How far do you think this will lead to the development and the opening up of trade from African countries to Europe and how far is the British Government pressing on that point? One of the documents we have got before us, which I think has been sent to us on the final communiqué of the troika meeting, says that ministers reiterated their strong interest in the development dimension of trade policies and negotiations, the need to support regional integration processes and the importance of access to the EU markets for products of export interests to African countries. I think the last is in fact very important, and of course David Cameron has been making a speech about it in the last few days. How do you see this developing and how far are we likely to get on it?

Mr Murphy: Of course, I did not have the opportunity to hear Mr Cameron's speech. I am sure it was interesting and with your Lordship's encouragement I will make time to read it.

Q3 *Lord Crickhowell:* I have only read a summary of it.

Mr Murphy: I did read some press coverage of it, but I have not had a chance to read the speech, but I will make sure that I do. In terms of the specifics—it may be helpful to your Lordships—there is a whole series of statistics in terms of the EU's aid effort, the agreement that was reached under the UK Presidency in 2005 and specific targets, different levels of financial commitment, of the 15 Member States, and then the others a smaller level of financial commitment. My understanding is that on those commitments from 2005 we are on track and I think the documents will talk about maintaining that trajectory to actually hit where we are actually aiming to get to. It would be helpful perhaps to provide those details to the Committee rather than reciting them, but on the specific point about the interplay between development investment versus the investment in the politics and the process that is needed to bring about a more effective trade policy, the Government's strong view is that these long-term challenges just will not be resolved exclusively through aid. It is about moving away from a governance arrangement which on some occasions seems to have the appearance of charity rather than self-dignity and the capacity for self-reliance. We all know that was relatively easily said as an issue of some controversy in UK politics a few years ago, but now it is largely established also in UK politics but it is much more difficult to deliver because it is not just about a bilateral and multilateral trade agreement, it is about properly functioning markets, the rule of law and the governance, the rule of law for foreign investors, a transparent regulatory regime and all those sorts of issues. So it is multi-dimensional, but we are committee to trying to achieve just that because that is the long-term solution for the continent of Africa and the individual states there.

Q4 Lord Anderson of Swansea: Minister, I wondered whether the Government has any thoughts about how to improve the so far not very impressive take-up on the African peer review group mechanism for looking at human rights, where a number of countries have volunteered to be submitted to this mechanism but an awful lot have not? It is highly desirable, I would imagine we would all agree, that more should do. Have we given any thought as to how we could—I suppose this is a slightly loaded word—"reward" counties which do submit themselves to the African review group mechanism, particularly countries which then implement the recommendations of the review group mechanism, because rather than talking about punishment of those who do not, it seems that rewards for those who do is perhaps the better way to go?
Mr Murphy: I put my pen down deliberately there because the one word that I had written down was "reward", so I do not think it was the wrong word. Perhaps we are both wrong in using that word, but it was certainly the word that I had scribbled on my notes. In the same way as in central Asia, which we may have an opportunity to discuss a little later, it is about, where we can, having tailored approaches to individual nations. Our aim is, insofar as it is in any way practically possible, to get as many of these

nations closer to international standards and the rule of law and the things I have already commented upon, but it is right that where there is specific progress and better than expected progress, or greater enthusiasm for progress, then there should be a degree of differentiation in terms of the UK's engagement and obviously the EU's engagement because I think that is a way of sending a very clear signal indeed in terms of what is appropriate in terms of the European Neighbourhood Policy and it is also appropriate in terms of the African Union.

Q5 Lord Swinfen: Minister, what is being done to help African nations improve their communications so that they can make contact with outside markets and their transport systems so that they can actually get their goods out?
Mr Murphy: In terms of the communications, one of the things that I am aware of from my previous role in Government is what more the international community can do working with some of the very big, for example, IT companies to ensure that what we now consider to be well-established communications systems—the internet, email, and everything else, which is the norm now, of course, in the international markets—is cleared for access for African business and African civil society and that some African states have the opportunity of lower cost access to some of that established technology, which has not been the case –

Q6 Lord Swinfen: They need good telephone communications, and they do not exist everywhere.
Mr Murphy: That is true. Your Lordship may know more about some of the specifics than myself, but certainly in some of the larger cities where they nevertheless do have well-established telephone systems, things like access broadband, a very large number are still relying on dial-up internet access rather than broadband access. Internet connections are often unreliable and email systems, where they are available, are only available to an elite and therefore it has not become the dynamic force for economic liberalisation that it can be in the proper context. There is an awful lot of that that has gone on, but I am sure in the case of most of these discussions more can be done. I have to be frank with my Lord that in terms of transport, I think that is about some of the investment with the UN programmes. It is also about—and this connects with the previous question—whether we can generate enough domestic tax revenue based on even marginally more dynamic market economies, which can lead to the type of domestic driven investment which ultimately is the solution. However, there is a substantial degree of UN commitment and World Bank commitment to invest in infrastructure, including transport.
Chairman: Thank you very much.

Q7 *Lord Lea of Crondall:* Our locus as a committee, Minister, as you will know, is where does the EU add value? We have discussed everything else, and it is all very interesting, but we are supposed to be looking at how the EU is going to add value. We spent the whole of last year, much of it anyway, preparing a report on the EU in Africa and there is now a pretty good correspondence between what the EU and the African Union countries have drawn up for the Lisbon summit and ticking the boxes that we recommended. I am not saying that has got any magical connection, but there is no doubt that our report was very widely received and the Portuguese have done a lot to pick up elements in it. Our central theme was, in case you thought we were slow to take the point, that in fact we can draw up as many checklists as we like but we cannot just transfer ownership of them. You cannot say a European strategy for Africa which is suddenly owned by the Africans, and that was a central theme. However, laborious as it was, there has been a lot of buy-in by the African countries and I want to come to the question of the European Union and the African Union per se. There is a lot of scepticism about it and even today there is only one man and a dog working on the Darfur dossier, whatever it is! But would you say that HMG, in the lead up to Lisbon, is thinking that we have got to still redouble our efforts in building up the capacity of the AU because on the governance questions, all the questions you have touched on, the governance questions, complex management questions, you cannot do this unless there is a credible and well-resourced and politically respected source of advice from Addis Ababa (if that is where it is) so that people do take on board governance and independent auditing and that no corrupt brother-in-law is running the Statistics Ministry and all the rest of it. So how does the AU as such fit in and AU/EU relations help to provide that framework?

Mr Murphy: Three quick points. One I have already alluded to, which is, as you have rightly yourself mentioned, it is about a proper partnership where we do not simply, in effect, as the African Union to simply sign a document that we have decided on their behalf and expect them to accept it. I suspect that possibly could be done if we wanted to. It should not be done, but it possibly could be done, but I do not think that is the route to delivering any content of the document. So while on occasion the process of getting genuine multilateral buy-in may on occasion blunt some of our ambition, it is important, I think, to get a document that people are determined to deliver. Of course, the European Union is the biggest contributor, but I think what would be reasonable for the African Union to expect from us as the biggest contributor in the context of the EU is predictability of funds. I think that is one of the criticisms thus far,

that it is a relatively ad hoc funding arrangement. If we ask for them to make a long-term political and civic society engagement in change, they have got to be aware that actually three years down the road the money will still be there, that there is money in place to deliver on the challenges that we agreed together, particularly if some of the leaders may be taking a risk in the context of domestic public opinion or the opinion of the elites round about them, to make sure that we are there with them and that it is sustained in a long-term way. In terms of the capacity of the African Union to deliver, I think the UK Government has got a realistic expectation both that the African Union can add value in terms of what it can do, and in the same way that it has got a realistic assessment of what the EU can do to add value, because ultimately that is the big question for the EU in all sorts of different areas, how does the EU's involvement add value in any field? So in terms of Sudan, Somalia and Burundi, the EU's investment is helping the African Union to make a real difference, but I am sure it is always the case that we can and could do more.

Q8 *Lord Lea of Crondall:* A lot has been stated about the huge jamboree in Peking last autumn and everybody went, 50 presidents, and so on. Do you think, now that the EU's approach with an awful lot of governance and perhaps, if not military cooperation, looking at the security side, and so on, and demanding certain things in terms of human rights, and so on, there is any sense in which you think the Chinese will have to start to go along with that in terms of their reputation, or will they just sweep up the resources like an ex-colonial power?

Mr Murphy: This is one of the age-old challenges, I think, and the UK through the EU insists, entirely properly, that partnerships must be based on relationships which respect and organisations which respect the rule of law, civic norms and international standards. While some are entirely appropriately and rightly doing that, but others, perhaps the Chinese, may exploit the map of opportunity and international relationships with a different approach. It is something we are conscious of, but it is our view that the way to actually deliver this kind of long-term change is not by the second approach. It does not deliver. A long-term relationship will be based on large parts of the two continents having a relationship based on a democracy, based on a mature relationship rather than a kind of opportunistic relationship. I think that is the way we see it.

Q9 *Chairman:* Thank you very much indeed. Perhaps I could just refer, while we are dealing with Africa and our own report, to something which we did not say we were going to ask you but which Lord

Grenfell wrote to you about and you replied, and that is of course the appointment of the European Union's special representative in Addis Ababa. As you know, we recommended this post should be double-hatted and we obviously have a considerable interest in this post in view of the fact that one of our colleagues may well be appointed to the post. We would obviously be very glad if you can keep us fully informed, as we shall wish to congratulate the noble Lady at the time of her appointment.

Mr Murphy: I was remiss, of course, in not mentioning that.

Q10 *Chairman:* Thank you very much indeed. I wonder whether I could go on to the Presidency report on the ESDP, which was considered at the European Council at the end of June. Among the discussions, rather interestingly, in that report there is reference to a European Union civil capabilities improvement conference, which will take place in November this year to discuss the improvement of the European Union's civilian capabilities for crisis management. I wonder whether you could tell us how the discussions on that are going, including whether there are going to be some new civilian headline goals for 2012 and what sort of obligations that might imply for the UK?

Mr Murphy: Just to update my noble Lords, work on the headline goals and negotiations have not actually commenced yet, primarily because of operational reasons and other commitments which exist. In terms of the conference and the updating process, one of the things we need to do is to learn from the increased experience which we now have in terms of missions. At the time of the agreement of the previous goals, I think we had only embarked upon three civilian missions. There have been many more than that now, and there has been a difference in terms of scenario planning and what actually then happened. The scenario planning had an expectation of commitment of personnel between 600 and 14,000, and that has been nothing like the case at all. The total commitment across the nine missions is 650 at the moment, so that has been a learning experience in terms of the scale. At an earlier point we overestimated the scale of the necessary commitment. There are wider lessons which have to be learnt, and in scenarios we tested a variety of these. The lessons we have learned, which should find their way into the new headline goals, are that there needs to be greater support from the Secretariat of procurement, greater central support and also better support of civilian support teams and better management and coordination of civilian support teams. There is also a medium-term issue of the coordination of civilian and military work based on this new set of headline goals, which would be possibly three years in duration, which would take us

to 2010, the military headline goals up to 2010. There will be an opportunity at 2010 to better coordinate civilian and military work. I hope, my Lord Chairman, you find that helpful.

Chairman: You have written to Lord Grenfell, and therefore to us, also telling us about the way in which the guidelines for the command and the control structure of the EU civilian operations are going to develop and that you are going to send us the precise amendment of the joint actions when they are agreed. Those sorts of advance notices are extremely helpful and I would just like to say thank you very much for giving us that sort of advance warning, particularly when there is a recess coming up.

Q11 *Lord Hannay of Chiswick:* The ESDP report called on the Portuguese presidency to take forward work on closer dialogue and cooperation between the EU and its partners in the field of crisis management, and it referred to the UN, the African Union and the OSCE. This brings us on to an area where the buzz word, I suppose, is hybrid operations because there is a lot of talk about that in the context of Darfur and there is clearly a similar situation (though in many ways different actors) evolving in Kosovo. Could you say, Minister, whether you think, apart from talking about hybrid operations, we are actually well-equipped in the EU to participate in them and to really work together with international organisations? As I am sure you are aware, the belief that international organisations actually cooperate well together does not survive five minutes in the field. They actually tend to cooperate very badly together unless there are structures and a very strong political hand behind them saying, "No turf fighting, please. Get on and actually work out solutions." Are you confident that the EU is well-equipped to regulate the kind of interface that there will be in Darfur, where it is likely to be a triple hybrid with an EU involvement, an AU involvement and a UN involvement, and equally complex arrangements in Kosovo?

Mr Murphy: First of all, on your own point, my Lord Chairman, about reports, I am glad that you feel we keep you well-informed, but if at any point you feel that is not the case it would be very helpful if you would let me know personally. On this issue of hybridity or the effect of multilateralism and whether we are good enough at it, my senses say no. Are we getting better at it? My senses say yes, and Lord Hannay will know from his own experience just in a practical sense the weaknesses and the feelings of previous hybrid operations. I do not think it is something that is in our paperwork today, but there is also the issue, of course, of NATO and the EU and NATO, the UN, EU and NATO, the OSCE and the AU, and everyone else. I am trying to think my way through. Conceivably the EU, NATO, the UN and there is also the African Union, but certainly the OSCE involvement, or a combination of some of those organisations and bodies. In terms of NATO there is the continuing difficulty about Turkey in terms of the sharing of information, the relationship in terms of NATO and the EU. In terms of the UN and the EU, the margins of the most recent G8, the UN and the EU signed a Memorandum of Understanding, and my noble Lord is aware of that. The expectation—and I put it in that sense—is that that would significantly improve the situation on the ground. In terms of Kosovo, as we move towards a diplomatic outcome—and we can talk later, perhaps, about what shape that diplomatic outcome will be arrived at—it is clear that the EU will have a really significant part to play, but also the OSCE in Kosovo, so that is a challenge, and the relationship depending on the exact mandate in Kosovo and the nature by which Kosovo derives its independence, of course, will determine which bodies on the ground are left with the responsibility on that crucial coordination in quite a tight timescale. So the short answer to your specific question, am I confident, is that I am confident we are getting better but I think we continue to learn, as the noble Lord is aware.

Q12 *Lord Hannay of Chiswick:* On the EU/NATO issue, do you not perhaps think, with the outcome of the Turkish election, the re-election of the AK Party Government with an overall majority and the commitment by Prime Minister Erdogan to resume the reforms and to press ahead with their application for the European Union, that this might be the moment at which we could revisit this really rather tiresome EU/NATO problem over the exchange of information which has come up because of the Cyprus/Turkey problem, and so on—not immediately, necessarily, but we really should not just simply sit back and take it as a given, because it is a real pain, frankly, and it seems to cause a great deal of irritation to all the players in Brussels?
Mr Murphy: My noble Lord is right, it is a pain and it hinders what should be a common sense approach to strategic cooperation. I think the Turkish elections do provide us with an opportunity, but obviously my understanding is that of course there are elections due in Cyprus within months, and I think once both elections have been successfully negotiated then that might provide the opportunity. But in the very short-term, I do not think there is cause for unconditional optimism, but post-Cypriot elections perhaps there may be.

Q13 *Lord Anderson of Swansea:* Minister, when in Bosnia the European Union took over from NATO the great advantage was that the European Union could deploy the multiplicity of tools in the toolbox ranging from both the military and the civilian. This is true, also, for example, in disaster relief operations where military helicopters will probably be needed to assist, and so on. Is it somewhat artificial to have a conference solely on the civilian capabilities when as important is the interface which the ESDP can provide between the military and the civilians?
Mr Murphy: As I said a little earlier, in the medium term this distinction which has built up over time, for whatever reason, is an opportunity in terms of a convergence of work plans on both to have common civilian and military headline agreements. Until then, I think we are working within the plan that we have inherited in terms of—I would not describe them as silos as such, but there is that need for the cooperation you are alluding to. In terms of the civilian work, it is about how we get there. The structure we have at the moment perhaps makes it a little more difficult, but it is how we properly coordinate the military support, support for police reform, support for judicial reform, support for the reform of civil protections, and everything else. Martin may wish to say a word or two about it, but by 2010 there is the opportunity for breaking down those barriers, but in the short term I am not exactly certain as to how that would work.
Mr Shearman: Yes, I think you are quite right, Lord Anderson. This goes back, of course, to when ESDP was devised, which was originally seen primarily as a military tool. Of course, since it was devised it has very much proven its worth as a civilian crisis management tool. I think 11 of the 13 missions have been civilian and the UK is a very strong believer in the need to try and bring these two tools together, and of course all the other tools which the EU has at its disposal. So I think a great integration of civilian and military approaches is something we will be aiming for. The recent developments in the civilian command structures in the secretariat in Brussels, which the Minister has written about, make some advance on that in that they bring more military planning discipline and more military planning advice into the process of civilian planning permissions, which I think is not a sufficient advance but is a small advance.

Q14 *Lord Lea of Crondall:* My Lord Chairman has referred to civilian and military, but I guess that everybody is trying to figure out the impact of moving from a position where you have got an EU High Representative for the Common Foreign and Security Policy and the Commissioner for External Relations. It has not been agreed—it has got to be ratified—that there will be one new High Representative. This could have quite far-reaching consequences in how the Commission and the Council of Ministers actually work together in this sort of way. Would you like to speculate about that?

Mr Murphy: I certainly would not invite Martin to speculate on that. I will not take my noble Lord up on his kind invitation to speculate publicly, but the fact is that this is not a change in the relationship on neither foreign nor defence policy in terms of the responsibility of Member States, despite what we may read in excellent national newspapers! The fact is that most people who have looked at this in any great detail assess it to be an intelligent way to have a more coherent single voice on these important issues in a way which does not jeopardise sovereignty, Member States' responsibility, unilateral responsibility or opportunity within multilateral organisations. I think it is a common, reasonable reform which should lead to great effectiveness.

Q15 *Chairman:* But it is the same person doing two jobs, rather than combining two jobs, and I think that distinction is rather an important one.
Mr Murphy: Yes.

Q16 *Lord Swinfen:* I want to move now to Central Asia. Does the Government consider that the EU's strategy on Central Asia is providing a good basis for meeting the goals of the EU's external energy policy?
Mr Murphy: I think it can do, but the energy markets and the interplay between energy markets, energy supply, public diplomacy and international relationships is of course always a complex one and our approach, as the UK and the EU, has to continue to reflect that. So the short answer is, yes, but we have to continue to remain relatively nimble, particularly in Central Asia. There are some specific challenges we still have to address. One of the big challenges is about the diversity of routes to market, for example. Your Lordships will be aware of the continuing issue of the perception—and the reality actually—of the EU's over-reliance perhaps on imported Russian gas. My understanding is that, for example on energy policy, specifically the UK on that matter is a 12% net importer of gas supply with very little from Russia, whereas the European Union imports about 50% of its gas, with 50% of the imports being from Russia. So the issue in respect of Central Asia is also about ensuring those issues of diversity of supply, and transparency of the market is important as well.

Q17 *Lord Swinfen:* If it was secure the political reasons would not just have the tap turned off?
Mr Murphy: I think it depends whose hand is on the tap and where these pipelines run through, and those are matters which the UK Government through the European Union—and incidentally the G8, because my recollection of the G8 process at St Petersburg was that all of those nations signed up to the St Petersburg declaration, which committed those states to an energy policy which had as its basis stability, transparency and predictability. The

important thing there for the UK Government, and I suspect also for the EU, is that that has been signed up to by all of those nations, including Russia. The energy policy and the dynamics of the energy policy have to be publicly delivered within that St Petersburg agreement. So what we now have to do, to my mind, is to make the St Petersburg agreement influence these individual tactical decisions and deals which are arrived at over the next few years. So I think the St Petersburg declaration is pretty crucial in that sense.

Q18 *Lord Hannay of Chiswick:* Meanwhile, is not the practice of the Russian Government not entirely consistent with the St Petersburg conclusions, because if one has understood it rightly the Russian Government's objective seems to be to ensure that Central Asian oil and gas, as far as possible, transits through Russia, i.e. it gives them a measure of control and to the degree possible, too, is under the control of Gazprom? That may not be in any legal sense against what was agreed at St Petersburg, but it is hardly within the spirit of it, and it is certainly not within the objective which the EU is pursuing of diversifying its supply, because basically it is concentrating more and more of the supply, including of Central Asian gas, funnelling through one very large country which lies in the particular part of the world that it does. Is there any way in which you think we can develop our Central Asian strategy to make it rather less likely that the Russians can pursue this policy even further?
Mr Murphy: Mr Parfitt may wish to comment a little on it, but one of the important things I think we can, and are, doing is pursuing an EU bilateral relationship with Turkmenistan, for example, as my noble Lord will be aware. From recollection, Turkmenistan is, I think, the third largest non-OPEC producer.

Q19 *Lord Hannay of Chiswick:* Yes, after Qatar and Iran, I think.
Mr Murphy: That is really very important in this context, but my noble Lord is right, there is a strategic decision taken by Russia of the importance of domestic supply and the routing of strategic pipelines. On the basis of the spirit of St Petersburg and in the context of a properly effective energy market, that may not cause many people to have a concern, it is a proper, transparent, effective free market in energy policy, but on the basis of some of the other dynamics within the energy market it does lead us in a determined effort to have a diversity of routes to the market, and that is really an important part of the EU plan in terms of energy. I do not know if Mr Parfitt wishes to add anything to that.
Mr Parfitt: I would only perhaps underline that, as the Minister has already rightly observed, much of this nexus of issues, it seems to me, boils down to the

investment climate which exists in the Central Asian region for the diversification which we and our Central Asian partners commonly seek to become a reality, and it is perhaps the absence of a sufficiently robust investment climate to date which has allowed Gazprom and the Russian Federation to have the monopoly which it continues to enjoy. Therefore, I think the Central Asian strategy is very much predicated on sending the message to our Central Asian partners that the EU is interested in seeing the correct investment climate being put in place in order to make this diversification a reality, but that certain of the Central Asian states need to take some concrete steps themselves in order to give market players the confidence to invest in very large infrastructure projects for that to happen.

Q20 *Lord Swinfen:* Is the EU prepared to put money up front?

Mr Murphy: The EU is prepared to help bring about the investment, but in terms of the intention of the EU it is also about them seeing a return for that investment. In the EU it is an investment of political and diplomatic will. Much of this is brought about, quite rightly, by private companies in terms of the investment.

Chairman: We are under some pressure of time, because I know you would like to be away about five o'clock, so I am going to miss the next question and ask Lord Crickhowell if he would like to ask you a question. Perhaps you might be able to send us a written answer, if you would be very kind.

Q21 *Lord Crickhowell:* How far does the EU strategy on Central Asia allow for the fact that many of the Central Asian countries, despite having Russian rule for a large part of the last hundred years, and so on, are very, very different in character, politically, economically and socially? Is Europe recognising that? We talk about these great areas on the map, Central Asia, as if they were all the same. How far is it recognised that we have got to actually have different policies for different states?

Mr Murphy: I think this reflects back on the conversation we had a little earlier in terms of the continent of Africa. Within the EU approach, the UK with others insisted that we did have a sensible tailored approach to different states in that part of the world. It will be a surprise to many, as my noble Lord referred to, after 80 years or so of Soviet rule to discover the sheer diversity in terms of culture and national characteristics that exists in that region. In terms of what we are doing, we are developing, where we can, a different approach to different nations. I already alluded to Turkmenistan, but if you look at the difference between Kazakhstan, Turkmenistan and Uzbekistan, in Uzbekistan we still have the EU visa restrictions and we still have the restrictions on

farm sales connected with the failing to make progress on human rights, whereas in Kazakhstan— back to this issue of reward, this issue of positive encouragement—because the market has been opened up there has been a strategic decision taken to have a different level of engagement as a signal to others that if they make the reforms which are necessary then it will lead to a change attitude from the European Union. So that is a process which should continue.

Q22 *Lord Lea of Crondall:* Coming on to Kosovo, Minister, there was a UN Security Council resolution introduced last week and there are two levels, I suppose, to the EU immediate prospects there. One is to do with the timing of the civilian EU mission, but could you put this into the context of the fact that it is a very sensitive time and the EU has got so many manifold interests and we want to give Belgrade some encouragement as well as a big stick if they do not cooperate? Could you put all that together?

Mr Murphy: I can try in the time that is available! In all of this we are absolutely clear what the end point is and it is independence for Kosovo. That is where we will end up. I say that first because I do not want in any way for it to be implied that the UK is in any way reneging on its responsibility, and we see it as a responsibility to the people of Kosovo. I met with President Ahtisaari earlier this week and went through with him again the detail of his plan and we remain very strongly of the view that his plan, because of the sheer work that he put in and the effort he made to try and find common purpose and common cause, should be the basis of the eventual settlement in Kosovo. In terms of the specific issue of the resolution of the United Nations, we intended to table with others a resolution which was relatively minimal in its demands and its specific content, but it was clear that that resolution was not going to proceed and as a consequence it has not been put. What we have now is, taking up the suggestion, I think originally by President Sarkozy, one more round of talks with the contact group. We are committed to doing that, but once that is concluded we then, as the international community, know we get to a really difficult decision which we cannot and should not avoid, because of our previous commitments and because of the situation on the ground in Kosovo. We have no intention of reneging on our responsibility, so it is pretty clear what are the options that are available to us, but our determination is still to give a resolution through the United Nations. At the end of whatever process we go through, we are clear that Kosovo and independence for Kosovo is the end point and not something which is continuously delayed. We are fast approaching a period where we do have to make the decisions.

Q23 *Lord Lea of Crondall:* Is it that Belgrade can play it by whatever the Russians are saying?

Mr Murphy: I am not party to the bilateral conversation between the Russians and Serbia, but there is a sense that President Ahtisaari's plan had an inbuilt reassurance for Kosovo and the Serbs in terms of protections of freedoms, substantial devolution and those sorts of protection. Our view is that while, of course, these highly sensitive issues, Russia's concerns have been met. Russia's legitimate public concerns have been met by President Ahtisaari's proposals and there is now no policy basis for us not to make progress. In terms of the specific status, in terms of the EU support on the ground, I think I am right in saying that 120 days after status has been agreed then there has to be an effective EU commitment on the ground. There is already an EU team in place now doing the preparatory work, which is another signal to the people of Kosovo that we are not reneging on our responsibility. I hope that puts some of the specifics together.

Q24 *Lord Anderson of Swansea:* So you agree that at some stage the moment of truth must come? President Sarkozy wanted a postponement of six months. It is said now that the US and the Kosovo President have come to a deal, in recognition of the US moving to their view, that they will postpone UDI, but Serbia has made its position clear, Russia has made its position clear, there will be no compromise, and within a short period of time, surely, the problem must be faced with all the consequences which Serbia has threatened?

Mr Murphy: The problem does have to be faced and the problem will be faced, but the end point is independence for Kosovo.

Q25 *Lord Hannay of Chiswick:* I do not want to criticise at all the decision which has been taken recently to postpone, as President Sarkozy has proposed. I think there is probably a lot of good sense in that but, Minister, could you perhaps reflect when the end of the 120 day period comes that it is sometimes better to force a country into casting a veto than to allow it to get away without ever having to veto, which is what the Russians have been allowed to do this time, because basically what we have done is to accept that because they told us privately they would veto it they do not have to sit there in the Council and reject what you yourself have rightly said, in my view, is a perfectly good set of proposals which take proper account of the Serbian minority, and so on. Next time round, I would have thought the balance of advantage may be rather different and flinching from putting a matter to a vote and compelling a country to veto is the best way of enabling them to get away with it with rather less cost than they would otherwise have to pay.

Mr Murphy: Without speculating in an unhelpful way, it is the case that we have committed to this one last round of talks. We come very shortly to a crucial international decision and without criticising the United Nations at all as an institution, it is the case that the people of Kosovo have been given a commitment by the international community and it is our intention, the UK and others, to help them achieve that. In terms of how we achieve it, we have not given up hope that there may be a UN route because there is not a substantial legitimate public rationale for rejecting in any substantial way President Ahtisaari's proposals. I made that clear to him again earlier this week, and we remain committed to doing that.

Q26 *Chairman:* I wonder if I could ask a final question, given the time constraints, and that is on the European Neighbourhood Policy. The June 2007 European Council invited the future presidency to take forward the work on the strengthening of the ENP. What progress do you feel has been made in the last year on the neighbourhood policy and what are the main areas in which the British Government would like to see further improvements?

Mr Murphy: There has been progress in the past year, and the German Presidency gave this some particular profile. There has been progress on Ukraine, on trade and with Lebanon and Egypt. The progress over the next period is primarily around the first high level conference which will take place, which will involve the EU Member States and those in the neighbourhood, both to the east and to the south. We see that as a really important gathering, the EU Member States, those in the EU's eastern neighbourhood and those in the EU's southern neighbourhood, a gathering of those governments and NGOs as well. The issues we expect to come out of that—and again it is about specifics—will be about governance, energy and the issue of economic liberalisation. But again it comes back to the point which has permeated much of our conversation today, which is about developing specific agreements with specific nations within different parts of our eastern and southern neighbourhood.

Chairman: Thank you. Indeed, the neighbourhood action plans, which are developed with partners, are important. We have just completed a report on the European Union and the Middle East Peace Process, which will be coming to you but which does in fact particularly talk about the way in which the neighbourhood action plan with Israel is something which is quite important in our relationship with Israel and indeed on possible leverage as far as our relationship with Israel in that situation. I would like, Minister, because I know your time is very constrained, to say how grateful we are. We had a question about strengthening the Mediterranean dimension of the ENP, which I know the Portuguese presidency is quite interested in and perhaps it might be possible for us to have a written answer on that. I would like to thank you very much indeed. It is a bit hard of you, because quite a lot of the things we have been talking about were things which really were developed and carried forward under your predecessor, but you seem, in the relatively short time that you have been occupying your position, to have learnt a great deal about what is happening. We certainly look forward to seeing you again and to talking to you on specific things. We have just started an inquiry into relationships between the European Union and Russia, and indeed last week we had Sir Mark Lyall Grant and two of his colleagues talking to us about the beginning of that inquiry. We will towards the end of it, because Russia comes within your remit as well, hope that we will have a chance to see you about that, but in the meantime I know that you have young children and as the Scottish school holidays began three weeks ago you really would like to get back! We hope you have a very happy holiday with them and we look forward to seeing you again in the autumn. Thank you very much indeed.

Supplementary Memorandum by Jim Murphy MP, Minister for Europe

QUESTION

The EU's Strategy on Central Asia (under section V) contains a commitment to "develop a Rule of Law initiative which addresses the specific priorities identified by each country". What are the main contours of this Rule of Law initiative, and what instruments, including financial, will be made available to implement it?

ANSWER

The objective of the Rule of Law Initiative in the EU Central Asia Strategy will be to work with the countries of Central Asia to promote legal and administrative reform to strengthen respect for the law by all levels of society thereby safeguarding both economic interests and human rights and fundamental freedoms. The Strategy aims to achieve this by providing training for countries in the region and the exchange of international expertise. This includes facilitating contacts with the Council of Europe's legal experts on the Venice Commission and seconding international experts.

We look forward to working with the Presidency, the EU Special Representative for Central Asia, the Commission and other Partners to develop the initiative, which we will want to focus on promoting the principles of good governance, economic reform including transparency of government, the independence of the judiciary, the safeguarding of human rights and fundamental freedoms and the security of contracts and investments.

Details have yet to be discussed, but possible instruments include existing EU Partnership and Co-operation Agreements with the Central Asia states, Human Rights Dialogues, the Commission's Assistance Programme and Member States' individual assistance programmes. The EU will also co-ordinate with other international donors, in particular the International Financial Institutions, the UN Development Programme and other relevant UN agencies, the OSCE and the Council of Europe's Venice Commission.

QUESTION

What plans are there for a strengthening of the Mediterranean dimension of the ENP?

ANSWER

The Portuguese Presidency is likely to attach great importance to the Euro-Mediterranean Partnership ('EuroMed'), especially on migration issues. However, the European Neighbourhood Policy (ENP) will remain a coherent, cohesive policy. The Portuguese have underlined that, while they will seek to develop a fresh approach towards the Mediterranean region, they will maintain a holistic approach to the ENP and intensify political dialogue with both Southern and Eastern neighbours. As I mentioned during our meeting, the Commission is organising a high-level ENP conference on 3 September in Brussels to which Mediterranean and Eastern ENP partners have been invited.

We believe that EuroMed should reinforce ENP aims of good governance and reform. We used our 2005 EU Presidency to push EuroMed towards more reform-oriented action and goals. As we approach the second anniversary of the Barcelona Summit, we want the EuroMed Foreign Ministers Conference (Lisbon, 5-6 November) to demonstrate tangible progress against the Barcelona commitments on political, economic and social reform, with clear targets for 2008, and follow-up to the EuroMed Code of Conduct on Countering Terrorism.

31 July 2007

ISBN 978-0-10-401159-1